From Abandoned To Above

Divannah Small

FROM ABANDONED TO ABOVE

DIVANNAH SMALL

From Abandoned To Above

Copyright © 2018 KDC Publishing

All rights reserved.

ISBN:

978-0-9858526-9-6

First Printing 2018

Printed in the United States of America

Published by

Unless otherwise indicated, scriptural quotations are taken from the King James Version of the Bible.

All Rights Reserved: All rights reserved under International Copyright Law. Written permission must be secured from the publisher to use or reproduce any part of this book, except for brief quotations in critical reviews or articles.

Divannah Small

From Abandoned To Above

Divannah Small

FROM ABANDONED TO ABOVE

DIVANNAH SMALL

A True Story of Healing, Deliverance and Transformation

From Abandoned To Above

Divannah Small

From Abandoned To Above

TABLE OF CONTENTS

Preface…………………………………………….2

Chp One – Before I Self-Destruct…………………9

Chp Two – Breaking Away………………………18

Chp Three – Persistence Is Key…………………28

Chp Four – A New Life……………………………39

Chp Five – A New Fight……………………………44

Chp Six – Defeating Goliath………………………50

Chp Seven – From Abandoned To Above…………60

Divannah Small

From Abandoned To Above

PREFACE

Divannah Small

PREFACE

My God, where do I even start with this. It's so deep and rich that it's crazy! And, all I know is *He* did it.

He really *did* do it for me! I had been bound and hurt for so long. Tormented. Just hurt. Locked up. Just locked up!

I don't even know what to tell you. All I know to tell you is *God* did it, and just believe God.

Please listen to me: Just..Believe..God!

He truly is a way maker and a miracle worker! And He *will* do it for you!

BEGINNING

I've been through so much, and all I ever wanted was to get out.

I just wanted to be happy. Whole and happy. Whole, happy and loved.

That's all I ever really wanted!

I felt like I had so much love within me, and I just wanted people to see it. To *give* it. And, to give *it* to me. I wanted to experience the love *I* had to give from someone else. Love was what I needed to fill the void inside of me.

Love: I needed it, I wanted it, I was desperate for it, my soul craved it and God was able. He did it!

Divannah Small

And now I know what freedom and true love is: Freedom and love is Him!

Well, now you're probably asking, "Well, how did you get it Sista?" I'm glad you asked.

I started off by writing and expressing myself to God; pouring out my soul, my heart, my mind and my thoughts.

I just needed this *thing* out – a release of some kind. Some of the things I wrote wouldn't even be addressed to God, but He still heard them. And man, I just thank God!

I *really* thank God!

BACKGROUND

Let me give you a little background.

As a young girl, even at toddler age, I wanted so badly to impress others.

From Abandoned To Above

Once when I was around age three, I remember eagerly washing myself up *by myself* in the hopes of impressing my mother by showing her what I had done – one of those moments like "Look at me, Mommy! Look at what I did and how much of a big girl I am!" Although her response escapes me now, her response is really irrelevant to the point I'm making.

> This became a pattern in my life: doing things I really didn't agree with just to please others.

I wanted so badly for others to be impressed by me. I was so desperate to impress and get approval from others until I did whatever I deemed necessary; and *of course,* what I did to impress people didn't end there.

Another time around age four, when I was living with one of my foster families, the children of my foster parents at the time wanted me to fight the other foster children. And of course, in order to get their approval, I did fight them.

Divannah Small

This became a pattern in my life: doing things I really didn't agree with just to please others.

I wanted approval, friends and people to like me. So, I did things to *get* that approval and validation from them.

SELF-WORTH

I even accepted people as friends in my life who didn't really value me as a person. People who were one way around me and another way around others, but who cared, right? At least I could say I had *friends*.

This was such a negative and unhealthy way of thinking. This also showed the low estimation I had of me.

I didn't really value myself, and it showed by the friends I chose and my willingness to compromise my own values to get or keep them.

I didn't really know my *true* worth. I didn't really know who *I* was; so, I tried to find my identity in people – being who and what *they* wanted me to be.

But, who was I really? Do you know who *you* are?

My Prayer is that, while you read this book, you are inspired by the stories I've shared; and that, wherever you lost hope, you gain it through recognizing and embracing God's love.

Let *Him* take you on a journey. And, through His guidance and wisdom, allow Him to rid you of all false perceptions of yourself, and bring you into a *true* knowledge of who you are to Him!

He loves you more than you know!

Chapter One

BEFORE I SELF-DESTRUCT

From Abandoned To Above

Chapter One

Before I Self-Destruct

In my intro I asked a question: "Do *you* know who you are?"

Deuteronomy 28:13 says:

> "...And the Lord shall make thee the head, and not the tail; and thou shalt be above only, and thou shalt not be beneath..."(KJV).

Did you hear that? God says we shall be *above only* and shall *not* be beneath!

Anything for which you compromise your self-worth and value is beneath you!

Divannah Small

Don't settle for *anything* or *anyone* that isn't God's best! You are a child of God and you are *above only!* Never forget that!

Thoughts Analysis

Every action and reaction starts with a thought. Have you ever taken the time to analyze your thoughts? What kind of thoughts do you have? Are they negative? Positive? Good at times, and then bad at other times?

Does what you think about build you up or tear you down?

Think about it: What's in your mental diet? What are you feeding and nurturing yourself with? Not only that, but who are you *allowing* yourself to be fed *by*?

Analyzing the thoughts in your mind is one of the ways you can find out what kind of mental diet you have and whether it is *destructive* or *pro*ductive.

Does what you think about build you up or tear you down?

What are the outcomes of your thoughts? And, what kind of actions do they produce towards yourself and towards *others*?

If your thoughts leave you miserable, depressed or hopeless, then you have a poor mental diet and your thoughts are self-destructive.

If your thoughts leave you upbeat, motivated or inspired, then you have a healthy mental diet and they are productive thoughts.

Anything that leaves you comfortless, depressed or without hope, does not come from God.

Anything that tears you down does not come from God. Remember, you are *above only*.

Proverbs 23:7 Says:

"...For as he thinketh in his heart, so is he..." (KJV).

Now, what is that saying to us? What we think in our heart is who we are.

Take some time and think about what and who influences the thoughts of your heart. Is it a friend, or a close family member? Maybe even a significant other? It all starts with your thoughts.

WRITTEN THOUGHTS

When I would write my letters to God, and even the letters that weren't addressed to Him directly, I poured out what was in my heart because those were my thoughts and my way of release...My outlet.

I had a destructive and derogatory way of writing. I expressed thoughts of anger and how I hated myself, my life and how it really didn't matter if I was around.

How my life was over and wasn't worth living because it was destroyed. I continually tore myself down.

I had a miserable and suicidal style of writing. And, if I didn't *write* those thoughts, I thought them, and on more than one occasion.

> Take some time and think about what and who influences the thoughts of your heart.

EXPERIENCES

Oftentimes, in my case, a devastating event and experience in my life produced these letters from me.

One experience happened to me around the age of 21 or so and left me feeling betrayed and like my life was over.

I would be extremely sad and depressed at times, although on the outside no one would ever know it.

I knew how to smile in public and cry behind closed doors because, on the inside, I was miserable and tormented.

Matthew 11:28 says:

> "Come unto me, all ye that labour and are heavy laden, and I will give you rest" (KJV).

Coming to God was the only way to get free of those negative thoughts and feelings I had.

Have you ever written a letter to God, or any letter in a diary or journal about how you felt concerning your life, yourself or even others in or *not* in your life?

Experiences can play a huge factor in how we view ourselves and what we think in our hearts about who we are.

What we allow ourselves to hear from others, and even what we allow ourselves to hear from *ourselves*, can have great influence on our ways or actions – whether destructive or productive.

In my case, *who I allowed myself* to be around and what *I allowed* myself to think about me showed in my self-destructive ways.

In the end, it is all a matter of choice. You can choose your friends, as well as your thoughts.

DON'T SETTLE

I remember a co-worker one time giving me really great and simple advice during a really hard time in my life. In so many words, they said "Just because someone chooses you doesn't mean you have to choose them back."

This was a great esteem lifter for me at the time during what I was dealing with. This saying let me know, as I interpreted it, that I didn't have to settle for less than what I deserved.

You don't have to settle for negative thoughts, or negative influences in your life. Remember, as I stated earlier, don't settle for anything or anyone that isn't God's best!

Are your thoughts God's best?

Are the people in your life *God's* best?

Are they *destructive* or productive?

Chapter Two

BREAKING AWAY

Divannah Small

Chapter Two

Breaking Away

What is the next step after you recognize destructive behavior in yourself? How do you detach yourself from something or someone you've been accustomed to for so long?

I remember when I first *wanted* a change and what *I did* to try and bring about that change.

Why do I say when I first *wanted* and what I *did*?

Well, first things first. After recognizing those self-destructive patterns in yourself, you must *want* a change; and then, at the least be *willing* to do something to show and prove that you truly want that change.

TESTIMONY

I'll give you my own testimony regarding this. First, as you can probably imagine, I did not always live a Christian lifestyle. Not even!

One characteristic of my behavior when I was younger was that I used to curse like a sailor; especially if you made me mad. Oh honey, you could believe it was over, and I was going to let you have it because you *asked for* it by making me angry! It was your fault, not mine! Does that sound familiar to anyone?

With that being said, I was very aware of my temper and ability to get angry, as well as my mouth

> You don't have to settle for negative thoughts, or negative influences in your life.

and how I could quickly go there with someone without much provocation; but, I was also aware of the fact that I wanted a change because I knew that behavior was unseemly and opposite the character of the *classy lady* I wanted to be!

OPPOSING BEHAVIOUR

For instance, I remember one time attempting to make an effort for that change one day by determining in my mind not to curse that day.

I was not going to curse for the whole day. I was determined!

I remember almost making it through the *whole* day until, when on my way home from work at the end of the day.

While on the Train and talking to my cousin on my phone, an elderly lady decided to chastise me and tell me, in a not so polite way, that I was being *too loud* on the phone.

Well, at that time, I didn't feel that I *was* too loud, and that did it for me! I let her have it, and freely told her how I could talk as loud as I wanted to; and then *purposely* started to talk obnoxiously loudly and let anyone else know on that train car that I was going to be as loud as I felt so long as I was paying train fare.

I did all this while still on the phone and talked about the lady to my cousin while she was still in my presence! In simple words, you can just say, I clowned.

DISAPPOINTMENT

I let her win – I cursed and all! I allowed her to provoke me to go there and get out of character.

In the end, though, I was disappointed because I felt I had been doing good that whole day; and then, *boom*!

Divannah Small

I let her get to me. I probably vented to my friend for about 30 minutes after the incident because I felt she made me miss my goal after I had gotten so far.

Even then, I felt that lady was used by the enemy to get me upset. But, in all of this, I still made an effort towards change because I truly *wanted it*.

Have you ever had a situation like this happen to you? Where you were sincerely trying to change and making a true effort? Don't give up, no matter the resistance that comes against you! God sees your effort and He knows your desire!

TIME

Ecclesiastes 3:1 says:

> *"...To every thing there is a season, and a time to every purpose under the heaven..." (KJV).*

This scripture says there's a season for everything and a time for every purpose.

Who do you think gave me that desire to want to change? And why? God did. Why? Because He had a purpose for my life.

> Don't give up, no matter the resistance that comes against you!

I wanted a change, and I could only do so much on my own. But, the desire and a willing heart was the fuel I needed towards getting the results I desired. God was answering my letters, or prayers, if you will. After this incident, other things started to happen and other desires for change started to come.

I remember in one of my letters asking God, in so many words, to take away the people and things in my life that He didn't want to be there.

Some of these things I asked of Him I knew would result in a painful, but much needed, separation if I truly wanted the change I desired. Negative influences had to go.

Divannah Small

DESIRE

At some point in time, between the age of 22 or 23, I no longer cared to go out to the clubs with my friends who I would normally go out with. And at one point in particular, I even remember having liquor in my freezer and refrigerator and knew that I no longer wanted to drink; so, I poured it out and threw the bottles away!

I also wanted to refrain from having sexual relations and threw away a box of contraceptives I owned.

All these actions were influenced by God. He got in my desires before saving me, and later filling me with the Holy Ghost.

The desire to do those things just left. Friends that I had had for years, I either had fall outs with, or we just stopped communicating. Toxic relationships were exposed.

God now had me on a different path. He was still answering my letters.

DECISION

James 4:8 says:

> *"Draw nigh to God, and he will draw nigh to you. Cleanse your hands, ye sinners; and purify your hearts, ye double minded" (KJV).*

This scripture is self-explanatory and tells us that, if we draw near to God, He will draw near to us. It then tells us that we are responsible for cleansing ourselves and purifying our own hearts.

So, how do we do this? As I stated before, it starts with first *truly wanting* a change, and then putting some action to it. And, what you are *truly unable* to do, God's power is able to help you.

I have always heard that God is a gentleman and He won't go beyond our own will. We must *want* Him;

and then, *allow* Him to change us, because we truly *cannot* do it *all* on our own.

Matthew 11:29-30 says:

> *"Take my yoke upon you, and learn of me; for I am meek and lowly in heart: and ye shall find rest unto your souls. For my yoke is easy, and my burden is light"* (KJV).

What we *cannot* do, we simply have to release to Him; and what we *can,* make the decision to do it.

All it takes is a desire and a decision.

Chapter Three
PERSISTENCE IS KEY

Divannah Small

Chapter Three

Persistence is Key

Just as this chapter is titled, persistence really *is* key: *Continual* action towards a desired result.

When you really want something, you must continually go after it. And if you truly have a desire for it, that desire will be what drives you to be *persistent* in reaching your goal.

PROOF

After I had made my decision to put action towards my desire for change, I knew the things I did towards getting that change could not stop there.

Now, I can't say it was easy every step of the way; but again, my desire is what drove me to keep going until I reached my goal.

After I stopped going to the clubs, drinking and refraining from having sex before marriage, my desire switched from wanting a change to wanting to be saved; and then I started to attend church.

NEXT

Thinking back, I remember when people would ask me what I believed in. My response would be something along the lines of "I believe in Christianity, but I'm not practicing it right now."

This was my response because I knew I was not living a *Christian* life; therefore, I didn't want to claim that I was a Christian. After all, I knew the things I was doing were not at all what Christians did.

I had grown up in church and was taught about God as a young girl, and I even believed in God, but I did not want to give myself the title of a Christian.

> When you really want something, you must continually go after it.

After stopping the clubs, the drinking, the sex...etc., God still required more after he took those desires away.

There are some things we need God's power to do because we cannot change them on our own; and then other things He requires *us* to do on our own.

Remember, God is a gentleman and He won't go past our own will.

He also won't put more on us than we are able to bear.

He *knows* what we truly *can* and *cannot* do or bear on our own.

PROCESS

Back to what I stated earlier, I started to attend church. I wanted to be saved and filled with the Holy Ghost.

Hence, to show God that I was serious, I started to get rid of some of the other things in my apartment that did not agree with the change I was trying to make and the new path I desired for my life.

From the teaching I received when I was younger, I knew that Christians dressed in a certain way and I had a lot of clothes that I knew were not very *Christian-like*. So, I went through them and got rid of a lot of those items that were not very modest.

Or, we can even say those items that were not church appropriate. Some of them even had the tags *still on them*; but, in the garbage they went!

GOODBYE OLD

I also went through my CD, book and movie collection and got rid of a lot of those too! I *loved* my music, but I still had to give that up too.

Anything that reflected my old world and lifestyle had to be given up if I truly wanted more of God, and He *knew* I was *able* to do it. Keeping those things around could have been a temptation for me to go back to what I was trying to get away from.

I truly wanted God; so, persistence and determination was key.

During this time of transition for me, don't think I wasn't tempted at times to do or keep the things, and even people, I needed to get rid of, because I was! But, my desire for God was greater!

> Remember God is a gentleman and He won't go past our own will.

I was determined to do whatever it took to get closer to God. Therefore, I had to be firm in my decisions.

NEVERTHELESS

1Corinthians 10:13 says:

> *"There hath no temptation taken you but such as is common to man: but God is faithful, who will not suffer you to be tempted above that ye are able; but will with the temptation also make a way to escape, that ye may be able to bear it" (KJV).*

Even though we can be tempted at times with things that are in us, God always gives us a way of escape.

I had a choice to keep the clothes, the CDs, the books and anything else I knew could tempt me into going back to what and who I no longer wanted to be; or, let go of those things and become who God planned for me to be.

I thank God I chose to let go!

Are there things in your life you're holding on to or refusing to let go?

What material possessions do you own that might be influencing you to stay the person you no longer want to be? Are you willing to let them go to get the change you desire?

Be firm, and remember, *persistence is key!*

DESIRE RECEIVED

Now, let me get back to my testimony.

As I got rid of the things that conflicted with the new path God had me on and continued to pursue after Him, He eventually gave me what I was looking for.

I remember going to a church at the time where they practiced tarrying on the altar of the church, calling on Jesus and waiting for God to fill me with His Holy Spirit

I had persisted in this on more than one occasion, but I was not getting the results I desired.

At times, I became discouraged and started to feel like something must have been wrong with me because God had not filled me with His Spirit.

I wanted to receive His Holy Spirit so bad, and felt I was doing what I had been told to do to get it. I even felt as if I was a good person.

[I later learned that my righteousness was as a filthy rag to God, and salvation wasn't something obtained by works or my own proclaimed righteousness; but, by faith, in addition to a broken heart and contrite spirit.]

Hebrews 11:6 and Palms 24:18 says:

> *"But without faith it is impossible to please him: for he that cometh to God must believe that he is, and that he is a rewarder of them that diligently seek him" (KJV).*

Divannah Small

"The Lord is nigh unto them that are of a broken heart; and saveth such as be of a contrite spirit" (KJV).

What is all of that saying? I had to first *believe* God, and then humble myself; knowing that no amount of righteousness I felt I had would *earn* me salvation.

It didn't matter how good I *thought* I was, because what and who I thought I was could not compare to *God's* righteousness. I was born and shaped in iniquity, and His righteousness could not be compared to the righteousness I thought I had.

I could never *earn* His love or His gift of Salvation. *Because* of His love, He *freely* gave it to me.

All we have to do is have faith in Him and diligently seek Him with a broken heart and contrite spirit.

With that being said, I was diligent and continued to seek Him *hard*.

And, if I wasn't filled with His Spirit at church, when I got home, I had service all by myself and had my own *tarrying* service, as they called it where I attended church at that time.

> Anything that reflected my old world and lifestyle had to be given up!

And eventually, God filled me with His Spirit right at home in the comfort of my own living room.

I will *never* forget that day!

I can remember everything being new to me. The outside was even different. *I* was different.

I was *new!* God had done it! He had really done it! He had saved me!

And, this was just the beginning!

Divannah Small

Chapter Four
A NEW LIFE

Chapter Four

A New Life

When I was initially filled with the Holy Ghost, I remember having some very powerful experiences!

NEW EXPERIENCES

One time, I remember waking up and then probably not too long afterwards, being pulled into a trance like state. I was given an open vision of me shouting (dancing) in the church.

I had a desire to praise God and dance before the Lord like I had seen others do numerous times but didn't quite know how.

Divannah Small

After this vision, I felt like God was telling and showing me my future and letting me know that this was going to happen.

It was so vivid and powerful until, when I came out of it, it felt like I had actually just finished dancing before the Lord by way of His Holy Spirit!

Convinced that this was going to happen, I awaited the manifestation. And, eventually, it happened!

I was loving my new life.

WALKING WITH THE LORD

Later on in my walk with the Lord, I came across a scripture that confirmed this type of experience:

Numbers 24:2-4 saying:

> *"And Balaam lifted up his eyes, and he saw Israel abiding in his tents according to their tribes; and the spirit of God came upon him. And*

> *he took up his parable, and said, Balaam the son of Beor hath said, and the man whose eyes are open hath said: He hath said, which heard the words of God, which saw the vision of the Almighty, falling into a trance, but having his eyes open: How goodly are thy tents, O Jacob, and thy tabernacles, O Israel!" (KJV).*

This was just one of the powerful experiences I had!

After this manifestation, I remember often being eager to get home after church just so I could have my own praise party.

I would turn on some John P. Kee and have me a good ole time – singing praises and dancing before the Lord around my apartment! Again, I was *loving* my new life!

And even now, God is *still* taking me on a journey.

God loves us so much, and He wants for all of us to experience His goodness.

GRATEFUL

> Convinced that this was going to happen, I awaited the manifestation.

I thank God for filling me with His Holy Spirit and giving me what my soul had been longing for.

God will truly change and fulfill your needs if you allow Him to!

Go after HIm and let nothing stop you!

Nothing!

Chapter Five
A NEW FIGHT

Divannah Small

Chapter Five

A New Fight

I was finally free from my past – Free from my old life! Free from the life and person that had kept me bound for so long.

There was nothing like *this* freedom, *this* happiness, *this* love, *this* joy!

After being depressed and tormented for so long, I was so happy not to feel sad anymore. I had dealt with depression and torment for so long!

I can remember when I had discovered I no longer felt the weight of it all. I remember telling that to one of the members of the church I was attending at that time over the phone after realizing it.

> The things I used to think about constantly no longer plagued my mind!

AH HA!

One day it just dawned on me that the thoughts I used to have and the things I used to think about constantly no longer plagued my mind! The power of God had destroyed that yoke of depression and torment in my life! My past no longer had the grip it once had on me because I now had a stronger force – the Holy Spirit – working with me, in me and *for* me!

And, I needed Him for this *new* fight I found myself now facing.

You see, although I had been filled with the Holy Ghost, I was still under attack by the enemy! And, even more so now that I had joined the Lord's side...anything to get me to go back to the life and world I had been freed from.

THE WARFARE

Talk about warfare!

The devil loves to play mind games with us and get in our emotions. Now that I was saved and filled with the Holy Ghost, my mind still needed to be renewed.

That mind renewing was only going to come by God's Word. So, I read my bible and got in the Word consistently; to not only fight against the wiles of the enemy and block his fiery darts he constantly shot my way, but to learn even more about God, His ways and get even closer to Him.

From Abandoned To Above

I never wanted to be separated from God's presence. Everything I had been searching for was right there in it, in Him, and I *never ever* wanted to be without it.

THE WORK

It wasn't always easy; but, with much prayer and resilience, I was able to overcome the attacks of the enemy.

> Everything I had been searching for was right there!

Two scriptures that helped me throughout the years to overcome and war against the devil's attacks were:

1) Luke 10:19, which states:

"Behold, I give unto you power to tread on serpents and scorpions, and over all the power of the enemy: and nothing shall by any means hurt you." (KJV)

and

2) 1 John 4:18, which says:

"There is no fear in love; but perfect love casteth out fear: because fear hath torment. He that feareth is not made perfect in love."(KJV).

These scriptures *really* helped me during my attacks. And, eventually, the demonic attacks happened less frequently!

GOD'S DESIRE

God does not want us to fear the enemy in any shape, way or form because He has given us power over him!

We are to keep him under our feet at all times! Remember, we are *above ONLY!*

From Abandoned To Above

Chapter Six
DEFEATING GOLIATH

Divannah Small

Chapter Six

Defeating Goliath

Ladies and Gentlemen, have you ever had something or someone that was extremely hard for you to let go of in your life, or hard to just stop thinking about period?

I know I did. Yes, before *and after* my Christian walk began!

Even *after* salvation, there were still some things I needed to get free of. Those things required a power greater than my own.

THE REAL STRUGGLE

Before my Christian walk began, there was a certain guy I was extremely crazy about.

I initially met him while driving downtown with a friend. That day, all of us as a group pulled over and exchanged numbers.

When I first saw him, I was instantly attracted, and everything went from there.

However, this guy was not a good guy for me to be attracted to. I compromised my values by associating with him, knowing my mother had brought me up far better.

I knew to respect myself and have integrity. But, with this guy, I found myself doing things I said I would *never* do. Never say never, right?

Divannah Small

AGAINST KNOWLEDGE

I knew this young man did not really care much for me; but, I told myself that, through my love, I could change his heart towards me.

In my mind, all he had to do was see and feel the love I had coming from me to know that it was real no matter the mistakes I had made in the past.

So, I compromised my values, allowed myself to be rejected, and degraded myself by giving him what he wanted to try and prove my love, eventhough I knew that wasn't good for me.

Not only before, but *during* my Christian walk, I thought about this gentleman.

I found myself not only harboring old photos of him, but also checking out his Facebook page, and looking through old messages between us. I did this because I still held onto his memory. I had not yet let it go!

ANOTHER CHANGE

> Even *after* salvation, there were still some things I needed to get free of.

One night, I remember having a dream where I ran into this young man. In the dream, we appeared to be having a casual conversation where we were briefly catching up on old times, and afterwards parted ways. Then, I woke up.

3 days later, I ran into the same young man that I mentioned earlier at a bank as I was rushing inside right before closing!

When this happened, I was bewildered because I had just dreamt about this young man. In fact, the same scenario in the dream happened at the bank!

I later revealed the dream to my Pastor and told him what happened. I found out that day from my Pastor that what I'd had was called a *night vision*.

Divannah Small

GOD'S PROVISION

God had *pre*pared me for that incident! And, that incident also let me know that I was free from the young man.

I know that not just women, but men also fall into this category – a category called low self-esteem or low self-worth. Oftentimes, how we view *us*, as well as how we believe others view ourselves is a result of being rejected somewhere in our lives; whether it was by someone in our childhood, or adulthood.

In either case, the results are still the same and play out in our behavior.

OVERCOMING RESIDUE

Dealing with and overcoming rejection was one of the greatest challenges I encountered in life!

From Abandoned To Above

This was something I struggled and was tormented with for over 20 years that resulted in much man-pleasing, feeling like I was unloved, not wanted and not worth it; so much so, that, even after salvation, many times I felt as if even God rejected me and didn't want me.

I was no good and a nobody. Something was just wrong with me.

Does this type of talk sound familiar?

Rejection can have a domino effect on your life. Not only does it lead to man-pleasing, depression and low self-esteem; but, it can also leave one holding on to the 'victim mentality.'

I had been through a lot in my life, and rejection was something I was more than used to. It plagued my life in more ways than one, and caused me to long for acceptance anywhere I could pretty much find it.

Low self-esteem caused me to degrade myself and even lose my integrity. Only God could help me overcome that!

Divannah Small

WEAPONS

One of the scriptures I was told to recite to myself in the mirror everyday once by my Pastor was Psalm 139:14 which says:

> "I will praise thee; for I am fearfully and wonderfully made: marvellous are thy works; and that my soul knoweth right well."(KJV).

This helped me to battle low self-esteem and see actual value in myself.

> That incident also let me know that I was free!

Another scripture that helped me was Jeremiah 29:11 which tells us:

> "For I know the thoughts that I think toward you, saith the Lord, thoughts of peace, and not of evil, to give you an expected end."(KJV).

This was a scripture that really helped me because I truly felt that God hated me at times.

I believe that, because I was still battling the spirit of rejection, the enemy had me to think the exact opposite of what *God* tells us He thinks toward us.

Other scriptures, such as Jeremiah 31:3, also helped me along the way, which says:

> *"The Lord hath appeared of old unto me, saying, Yea, I have loved thee with an everlasting love: therefore with lovingkindness have I drawn thee."(KJV).*

This scripture also helped me when I need to be reminded of the kind of love God had towards me; and it still helps me today!

EVERLASTING

God's love is an everlasting love! He will never leave us or forsake us!

If you struggle with any of the things I've mentioned in this chapter; or, even anything remotely close to it, my prayer is that God reveals and allows you to feel *His* love for you!

> This helped me to battle low self-esteem and actual value in myself.

That He destroys the *lies* that have been built in your mind through all the years of rejection and/or abuse you may have suffered.

Ask God to show you who you are to Him.

Remember, His thoughts of us are thoughts of peace, and *not* of evil, to give us an expected end!

Your latter *will* be greater than your past!

Chapter Seven

FROM ABANDONED
TO ABOVE

Divannah Small

Chapter Seven

From Abandoned to Above

My life, from childhood to adulthood – which started out in the projects on the West Side of Chicago, to the shelters, then the foster homes, and later to adoption – seemingly had been a life of turmoil and appeared as if the odds were just against me!

But, I *now* know that *everything* I went through had a purpose. I became a *victim* to become a *victor*, and it was all in God's plan!

A lot of things that happen to us in our lives are not for us to be bound by them and remain victims of what we went through, but to overcome them and become *victor*ious! We then can tell someone else who may be going through that very *same* or *similar* thing that once had us bound that they may *also* come out!

I don't care what it is you've been through in life, and no matter how horrible it may seem, know that you *can* make it through *ANYTHING* with the Lord on your side!

THANKFUL

I thank God for a new life! What the enemy meant for evil God has surely used it for my good!

It has truly made me into the woman I am today. I don't regret anything I've gone through, no matter how painful *or* shameful.

In it all, I'm truly just glad to be saved! I'm glad that God *saw* something *worth* saving! As the song says: "*...He thought I was worth saving...*" (smile).

CONCLUSION

I pray this book has blessed and encouraged you in some shape, way or form, as well as given you some direction and guidance in receiving the healing your mind, heart and soul has been or may be longing for!

No one knows your story, understands and feels your pain in depth like God does. So, allow Him to free you like no one else can.

Holding on, often, is easier than letting go when we have been accustomed to something for so long. We fear change, or even our minds are just conditioned not to believe and expect the worse.

But, give God a try! *Trust* Him and see won't He go *past* your expectations. He's able!

I don't regret anything I have gone through, no matter how painful or shameful.

From Abandoned To Above

Divannah Small

ABOUT THE AUTHOR:

Divannah Small has a heart and passion for helping young women become whole in every area of their lives to reach their maximum potential.

Divannah believes in loving God and learning *how* to let God love you.

Divannah has overcome obstacles, failures and mistakes along her life's journey, and doesn't mind sharing her experiences for others to learn and grow toward their successful life.

Divannah resides in Chicago with her husband Aaron Small, Jr. and their daughter Hannah.

FOR BOOKING:
Divannah Small
Phone: (872)903-3587
Email: Divadams04@gmail.com

KDC.ENTERPRISES

From Abandoned To Above

www.ingramcontent.com/pod-product-compliance
Lightning Source LLC
Chambersburg PA
CBHW020702300426
44112CB00007B/488